LOVELIGHT MAGIC

Colette Fischer

June 23, 2021

Dear Julian,
May your lovelight
shine brightly out
into the world!
~lovelight~
Blessings
♡Colette

Published by:

Jasmine Moon Press

jasminemoonpress.com

ISBN-13: 978-0615951720
ISBN-10: 0615951724

LCCN: 2014930867

Credits

Cover Design by Colette Fischer
Photography by Petra and Dan Campanelli; Maggie Brubaker
Interior Layout by Gary A. Rosenberg

10% of the net proceeds from each book sale are dedicated to an annually selected orphanage worldwide.

This book is dedicated to children spanning the globe,
all of whom are bathed in the rays of the sun and
cradled to sleep under the same watchful eye of the moon.
To children both near and far, who shimmer in all the
colors of the rainbow, healthy or sick, wealthy or poor,
happy or sad, remembered or forgotten, lonely or not.
May the *lovelight* within you be nurtured and may it
cast a protective, loving glow that transcends all.

Do you know that I am filled
with magic?

And so are you?

I have a lovelight.

Just like you do, too.

My lovelight is a special gift,

a part of the universe all around;

a part of me so sacred,

it guides me without making a sound.

It lives in a precious place

and is lovingly known to me;

it is a part of my spirit,

which I can share with all,
you see.

When I take a giant breath

and close my seeing eyes,

I can draw deep inside
my-lovelight-self,

where answers come easily
without disguise.

And when I let my lovelight shine,

and it glows with happiness and delight,

I clearly see the path to all that is good,

whether it is day or the darkest dark
of night.

And if I feel sad and lonely,

or sometimes a wee bit blue,

I nudge my lovelight to sparkle
and glisten,

blanketing me with fresh
love-droplet dew.

The streaks of silver then
shining from my heart

make for a smiling feeling
and sight;

those around me cherish
its magic,

and kindle their own lovelights
with speedy might.

One light lights another,

and so the flame of love begins
to grow.

Its heat is made up of kindness
and respect,

enveloping earth in its brilliant glow.

No matter how small you
or I might be,

a loving light makes for a whale
of a snuggly feel.

Give in to its tenderness

to unleash a power true and real.

With a sprinkle of stillness
in your thoughts,
seek the lovelight in your heart.

It is always there for you,
faintly whispering right from wrong
in all that you do.

Our wondrous world depends on us
to shower all with peace,

to behold a beauty so precious
and rare,
unlocked by our very own
lovelight keys.

"May you always remember the lovelight in your heart. Nurture it, and take it out into the big, wide, beautiful world."

Colette Fischer resides in Colorado with her husband and two sons, who inspired *Lovelight Magic*. The splendor of the Rocky Mountains warms their spirit and beckons them to explore throughout the seasons, rain, snow or shine. In their free time they can be found camping, hiking, skiing, or biking.